Boreal Forest Animals

Biome Beasts

Lisa Colozza Cocca

Rourke
Educational Media

A Division of
Carson
Dellosa
Education

rourkeeducationalmedia.com

ROURKE'S
SCHOOL to HOME
CONNECTIONS
BEFORE AND DURING READING ACTIVITIES

Before Reading: *Building Background Knowledge and Vocabulary*

Building background knowledge can help children process new information and build upon what they already know. Before reading a book, it is important to tap into what children already know about the topic. This will help them develop their vocabulary and increase their reading comprehension.

Questions and Activities to Build Background Knowledge:

1. Look at the front cover of the book and read the title. What do you think this book will be about?
2. What do you already know about this topic?
3. Take a book walk and skim the pages. Look at the table of contents, photographs, captions, and bold words. Did these text features give you any information or predictions about what you will read in this book?

Vocabulary: *Vocabulary Is Key to Reading Comprehension*

Use the following directions to prompt a conversation about each word.

- Read the vocabulary words.
- What comes to mind when you see each word?
- What do you think each word means?

Vocabulary Words:
- camouflage
- climate
- defrost
- hibernation
- insulation
- migrate
- prey
- scales
- traction
- tundra

During Reading: *Reading for Meaning and Understanding*

To achieve deep comprehension of a book, children are encouraged to use close reading strategies. During reading, it is important to have children stop and make connections. These connections result in deeper analysis and understanding of a book.

 Close Reading a Text

During reading, have children stop and talk about the following:

- Any confusing parts
- Any unknown words
- Text to text, text to self, text to world connections
- The main idea in each chapter or heading

Encourage children to use context clues to determine the meaning of any unknown words. These strategies will help children learn to analyze the text more thoroughly as they read.

When you are finished reading this book, turn to the next-to-last page for **Text-Dependent Questions** and an **Extension Activity**.

Table of Contents

Biomes

Earth's surface is divided into large areas called biomes. Each biome has a certain **climate** and living things within it. The plants and animals there have adapted to life in that area's climate.

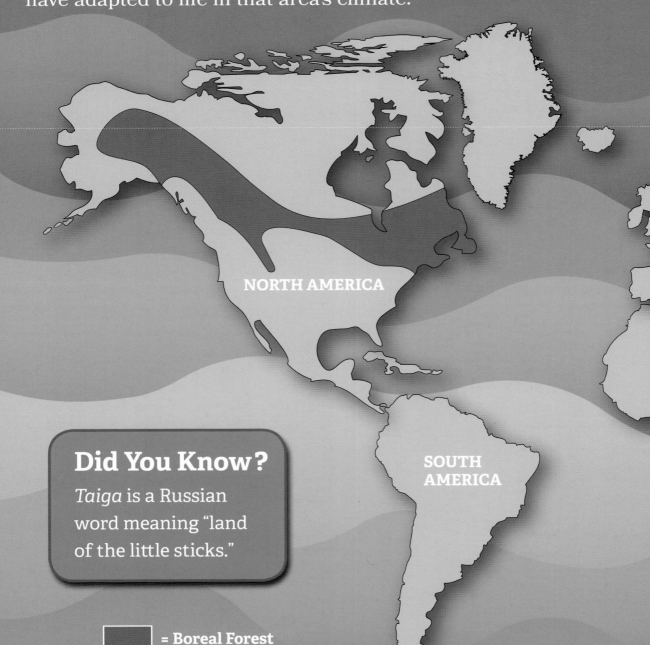

NORTH AMERICA

SOUTH AMERICA

Did You Know?

Taiga is a Russian word meaning "land of the little sticks."

= Boreal Forest

The boreal forest, also known as the taiga, is the largest land biome. It stretches across northern areas of North America, Europe, and Asia. This band of forest borders the Arctic Circle.

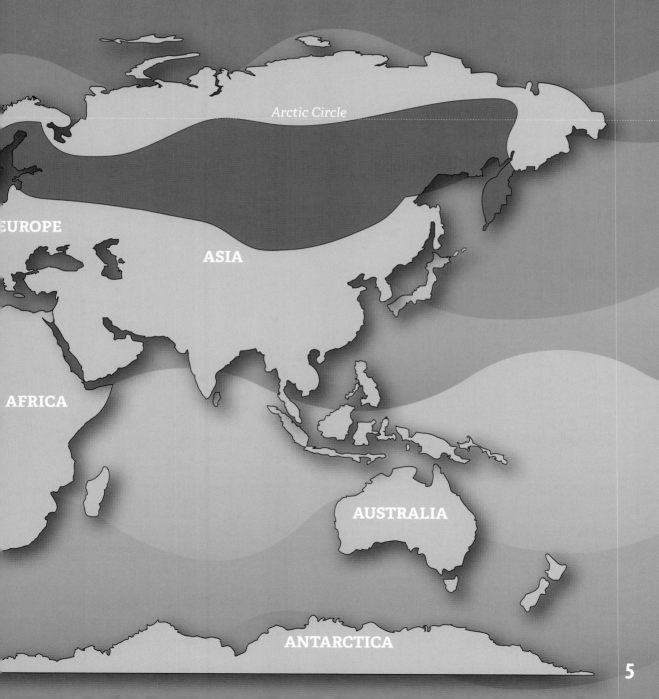

Arctic Circle

EUROPE

ASIA

AFRICA

AUSTRALIA

ANTARCTICA

The boreal forest biome has a cold, wet climate. It is second only to the **tundra** in coldness. Summers in the forest are short and rainy with temperatures ranging from cool to warm.

Winters are very cold and snowy. Temperatures can drop down as low as -85° Fahrenheit (-65° Celsius). There are only 50 to 100 days each year without frost.

Most of the forest is made up of conifer trees, which are trees with needles and pine cones. The waxy covering on the needles slows water loss. This is important when the ground is frozen. The dark color of the needles helps the trees absorb more of the sun's heat energy.

Even the pointy shape of the conifer tree is important to its survival. Because of its shape, snow slides off the branches. This helps prevent the cracking and loss of branches.

Did You Know?

The boreal forest covers about 17 percent of Earth's surface. Few people live here. Less than .005 percent of the world's human population calls the boreal forest home.

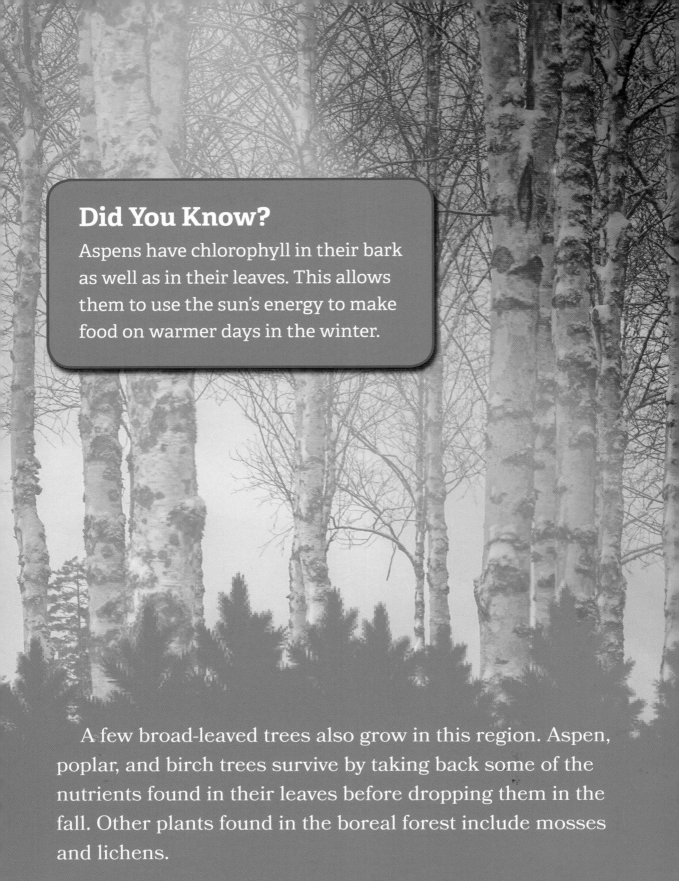

Did You Know?

Aspens have chlorophyll in their bark as well as in their leaves. This allows them to use the sun's energy to make food on warmer days in the winter.

A few broad-leaved trees also grow in this region. Aspen, poplar, and birch trees survive by taking back some of the nutrients found in their leaves before dropping them in the fall. Other plants found in the boreal forest include mosses and lichens.

Migration

The animals that are part of the boreal forest biome must survive the climate and the limited variety of plant life. Many animals spend only part of the year here. In the spring, the bogs, ponds, and lakes in the region become breeding spots for insects. Billions of birds **migrate** to the forest to feast on these bugs and the fish in the water.

Warblers, thrushes, loons, Canadian geese, and trumpeter swans nest and breed here. By fall, they migrate south.

magnolia warbler

trumpeter swan

loon

Caribou follow the opposite migration pattern. They leave in the spring and head north to the tundra. In the fall, they return to the boreal forest where they can find a supply of lichen to eat.

Hibernation

Hibernation is another survival behavior. During hibernation, an animal's heartbeat, metabolism, and breathing slow down.

Marmots are rodents that live in burrows underground. In the summer, their bodies store extra fat for energy during the winter. In the fall, the marmots dig deeper burrows. About 15 marmots share a burrow, which helps the rodents keep warm. They hibernate for about eight months of the year.

Did You Know?

Jumping mice hibernate all winter. In the boreal forest, these mice are about 12 percent bigger than jumping mice in other biomes. Their size gives them extra protection from the cold.

Before the ponds and lakes freeze over, snapping turtles dive to the bottom of the water and burrow into the mud. The mud acts like a blanket. It lowers heat loss in the turtles while they hibernate for about six months.

Did You Know?

Garter snakes hibernate in large groups. Hundreds of garter snakes share a single underground burrow for the winter. Hibernation allows them to be one of the few reptiles that can live in the boreal forest year-round.

Wood frogs have a unique adaptation to the cold. A wood frog hibernates under a blanket of plant materials and snow. In the coldest weather, the frog's body will partly freeze. It may freeze and slowly **defrost** several times during its eight-month hibernation.

The boreal forest is also home to brown, black, and grizzly bears. The bears gain extra fat for the winter. They do not hibernate, though. Their heart rates do not slow down enough for a true hibernation. Instead, they sleep through the winter. The bears sometimes wake for short periods and leave their dens.

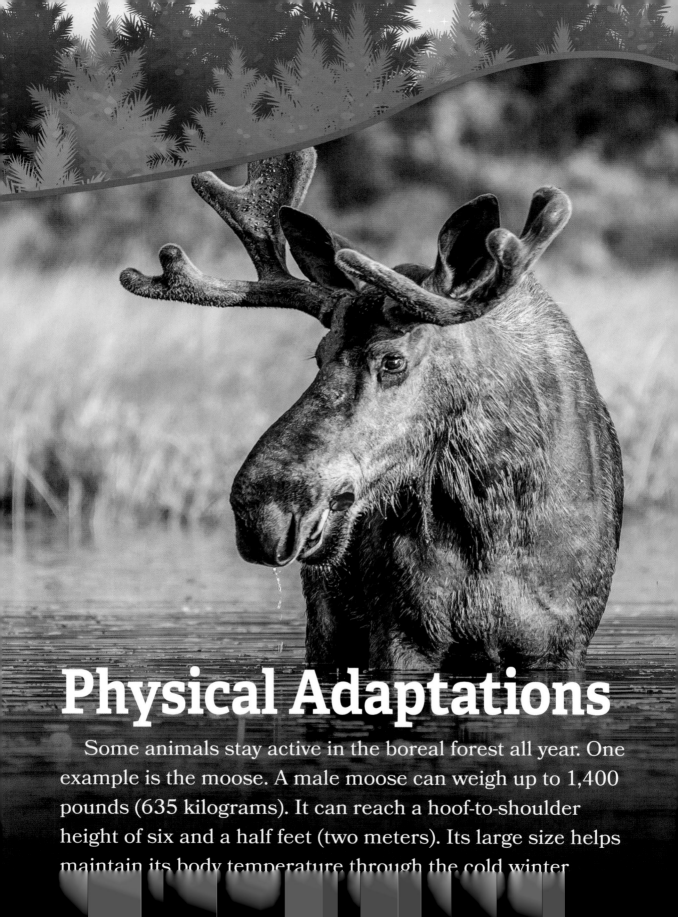

Physical Adaptations

Some animals stay active in the boreal forest all year. One example is the moose. A male moose can weigh up to 1,400 pounds (635 kilograms). It can reach a hoof-to-shoulder height of six and a half feet (two meters). Its large size helps maintain its body temperature through the cold winter

The moose's long, thin legs are perfect for plowing through tall snowdrifts. Its hooves act like snowshoes to keep the moose from sinking into snow or mud.

Did You Know?

Like many other boreal beasts, wolves have thick fur coats for warmth in the winter. Their sharp claws and the large, fleshy pads on their paws help them grip and maintain balance on snow.

Wolverines are a kind of weasel. Their dark, oily fur resists water and frost. When a wolverine walks, its paws spread out to about twice their original size. This makes it easier to walk on snow.

Wolverines use their excellent hearing to hunt at night. They can burrow under the snow to catch voles and other rodents. They can also move quickly on snow to catch bigger **prey** such as deer, sheep, and small bears.

Woodpeckers, finches, nuthatches, chickadees, owls, grouse, and ravens are birds that remain in the boreal forest all year.

The black-capped chickadee has a black and white feather pattern. This helps the feathers absorb heat and provide **insulation**. The bird sleeps in holes in the snow. The snow hole acts like an igloo and helps keep the bird warm.

A crossbill is a kind of finch. Its special beak allows the bird to find food in the forest all year. The lip of each half of the bill crosses over the other half. The bird uses its special bill to pry apart the **scales** of a pine cone to get to the seeds.

Super Senses

Some animals use their super senses to survive in the boreal forest. Great gray owls have extremely sensitive hearing. As they swoop down over land, they can hear voles and other rodents moving below the snow. They break through the snow and capture their prey.

Did You Know?

A lynx's long, thick winter coat covers its whole body—even its feet! Retractable claws improve its **traction** on the snow. Excellent hearing and eyesight make it a skilled hunter that can find and catch prey year-round.

A snowshoe hare's sharp hearing helps it avoid predators, including lynx, foxes, bobcats, and great horned owls. But that is only one of the adaptations that help it stay active all year in the boreal forest. The hind legs, feet, and toes on a snowshoe hare are larger than on other hares. This makes movement on snow and ice easier.

The hare's thick brown fur blends into the trees and grasses in the spring. In the winter, the fur turns white so it can blend into the snow! This **camouflage** helps the hare hide from predators.

The boreal forest is a challenging place for the animals that live there. They must find ways to adapt to its short summers and harsh winters. For some, seasonal migration or hibernation is the solution. Others rely on physical adaptations such as increased size, thick fur, color changes, and extra-sensitive hearing in order to be a part of this northern biome.

ACTIVITY: Heat Experiment

Look back at the pictures in this book and read the descriptions of the animals. Notice the color of their fur or feathers during winter. Then, complete this experiment.

Supplies

- six sheets of construction paper: one each of black, white, red, blue, green, and yellow
- tape
- pencil and paper
- six thermometers

Directions

1. Fold each piece of construction paper in half lengthwise.
2. Tape the bottom and the long side shut, creating a tall envelope.
3. Make a chart with a row for each envelope color and columns for recording temperatures.
4. Decide which thermometer you will put in each envelope. Use the first column on your chart to record the temperature on the thermometer before you put it inside the envelope.
5. Place the envelopes a few inches apart from each other on a flat surface in a sunny location.
6. Read and record the temperature inside each color envelope every 15 minutes for two hours.

In which colors did the temperature rise the fastest? In which colors did the temperature rise the most? How can the color of an animal's fur help it survive in harsh winter areas like the boreal forest?

Glossary

camouflage (KAM-uh-flahzh): coloring that allows animals to hide by looking like their surroundings

climate (KLYE-mit): weather of a particular region over a long period of time

defrost (di-FRAWST): to go from a frozen state to a non-frozen state

hibernation (HYE-bur-nay-shuhn): a period of deep sleep during which an animal's heart and lungs slow down to save energy

insulation (IN-suh-lay-shuhn): a covering to keep heat from escaping

migrate (MYE-grate): to move from one region to another

prey (pray): an animal that is hunted for food

scales (skaylz): thin, overlapping pieces

traction (TRAK-shuhn): the sticky friction force that allows a body to not slip as it moves across a surface

tundra (TUHN-druh): a very cold, treeless region on the surface of Earth

Index

Text-Dependent Questions

1. How do conifer trees survive in the boreal forest?

2. Why do caribou migrate?

3. How is the winter behavior of a bear different from true hibernation?

4. Why do black-capped chickadees dig holes in the snow?

5. Why is a great gray owl's hearing important to its survival in the winter?

Extension Activity

What advice would you give to someone planning to hike and camp in the boreal forest? Write a blog post explaining to adventurers how to prepare for the conditions they will find there.

About the Author

Lisa Colozza Cocca has enjoyed reading and learning new things for as long as she can remember. She lives in New Jersey by the coast. She is always cold so she probably would not do well in the boreal forest! You can learn more about Lisa and her work at www.lisacolozzacocca.com.

© 2020 Rourke Educational Media

www.rourkeeducationalmedia.com

PHOTO CREDITS: Cover: ©Richard Seeley, ©AnttiPulkkinen, ©Torence Hayes, ©Sonya_illustration; page 3: ©Sonya_illustration; page 6: ©Robert St Piere; page 7: ©TT; pages 8-9: ©donald_gruene; page 8b: ©Elena Shutova; page 10: ©Binnerstan; page 11: ©Sharply_done; page 12-13, 28: ©Eerik; page 12a: ©Glass and Nature; page 12b: ©Tammy Wolfe; page 12c: ©DChovi; page 13: ©Agnieszka Bacal; pages 14-15: ©Brian Ekushner; page 15: ©Creative Nature_nl; page 16: ©EEI_Tony; page 17: ©Jason Ondreicka; page 17b: ©MGJdeWit; page 18: ©Erik Mandre; page 19: ©Mark Byer; page 20: ©C_Gana; page 21: ©Andyworks; pages 22-23: ©Anna Yu; page 24: ©Alain Masse; page 25: ©BirdInages; page 26: ©Kaido Karner; page 27: ©Seventh Day Photography; page 29,30,31,32: ©Lonely_

Edited by: Kim Thompson
Cover & Interior design by: Kathy Walsh

Library of Congress PCN Data

Boreal Forest Animals / Lisa Colozza Cocca
(Biome Beasts)
ISBN 978-1-73161-439-1 (hard cover)
ISBN 978-1-73161-234-2 (soft cover)
ISBN 978-1-73161-544-2 (e-Book)
ISBN 978-1-73161-649-4 (ePub)
Library of Congress Control Number: 2019932139

Rourke Educational Media
Printed in the United States of America,
North Mankato, Minnesota